fast fun & easy

HOME ACCENTS

15 Fabric Projects to Decorate Any Space

Pam Archer

C&T PUBLISHING

Pam Archer

C&T Publishing

Text © 2006 Pam Archer

Artwork © 2006 C&T Publishing

Publisher: Amy Marson

Editorial Director: Gailen Runge

Acquisitions Editor: Jan Grigsby

Editor: Cyndy Lyle Rymer

Technical Editors: Elin Thomas and Susan Nelson

Copyeditor/Proofreader: Wordfirm Inc.

Cover Designer: Kristy K. Zacharias

Design Director/Book Designer: Kristy K. Zacharias

Illustrator: John Heisch

Production Assistant: Matt Allen

Photography: Diane Pedersen and Luke Mulks unless
    otherwise noted

Published by C&T Publishing, Inc., P.O. Box 1456,
    Lafayette, CA 94549

Library of Congress Cataloging-in-Publication Data

Archer, Pam Kincaid

Fast, fun & easy home accents : 15 fabric projects to decorate any
space / Pam Archer.

p. cm.

ISBN-13: 978-1-57120-324-3 (paper trade)

ISBN-10: 1-57120-324-9 (paper trade)

1. Textile crafts. 2. House furnishings. 3. Interior decoration. I. Title:
Fast, fun & easy home accents. II. Title.

TT699.A73 2006

746—dc22

2005022316

Printed in China

10 9 8 7 6 5 4 3 2 1

Dedication

This book is dedicated to my Dad, William A. Horning. Your strength, love, and words of encouragement and wisdom live on.

Acknowledgments

To the C&T family—Cyndy Rymer, Diane Pederson, Jan Grigsby, and Amy Marson—thank you all for your words of wisdom and support during this creative endeavor.

Jean Chandler and Sarah H. Lajoie, thank you for your uncondi-tional friendship, candor, and "therapeutic" walks.

My thanks to Marsha McClintock and Barbara Weiland, for your friendship, support, and guidance.

To the Portland "Dream Team"—a fabulous group of well-known fabric artists that I am honored to be a part of—many thanks for your insights shared, expertise, and support.

A special thank you to Linda Griepentrog.

To the wonderful men in my life, Mike, Scott and Brent Archer and my brothers, Fred and Bill—your support, insights and humor sustain me.

Thanks Mom, for your constant instrumental love and guidance.

Many thanks to Nancy Jewell and the staff at Husqvarna Viking, for their support and use of their wonderful Viking Designer 1 Sewing Machine.

Contents

setting a mood
with fabric

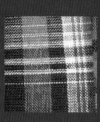

You know you're home when you walk in the door and feel at ease. The environment you created welcomes you home. Your eye travels effortlessly through the room.

It suggests a certain comfort and familiarity—all communicated by interesting textures, inviting colors, and a cohesive theme. You can easily add these elements by sewing your own simple projects.

Your home is the perfect place to reflect your preferences and unique personality. This becomes an easy task if you know what you like. But what happens when you are not sure of your preferences? How do you find that "just-right blend" that communicates the uniqueness of your space?

There are many ways to develop a room's look. Begin by looking at the intended function. For example, a bedroom calls for tranquility; a sewing room requires working space and good lighting; a dining room should be easy care. Add the desired *feel* of the room to the mix. For instance, a powder room might convey femininity, while the den may require a more masculine approach.

Once a room's function and feel have been determined, there are additional considerations. Is a fresh coat of paint needed to change the mood? Does the furniture need to be rearranged to create a more pleasant traffic flow? Sometimes it's as simple as pulling together a few accessories to add a dimensional layer of interest.

Say It With Color

Color plays an important role in home décor sewing. When one color is paired with another, it becomes a color scheme that determines the room's theme.

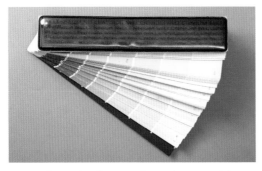

Painter's palette—a decorating essential

Whether your room calls for a complete color makeover or harmonizing a few accessories, a quick review of color theory will help you on the way to success.

color theory 101

A color wheel or the 3-in-1 Color Tool (see Resources) is a valuable sewing and decorating tool to ease the color selection process.

3-in-1 Color Tool

Here are a few tips to keep in mind when considering color choices.

☐ Light colors advance, making things appear larger. Dark colors fool the eye into believing that things are smaller than they really are.

☐ Yellow-based colors are referred to as warm; blue-based colors are cool.

☐ Gray, black, beige, and white are all considered neutrals. These basic shades pair up readily with other colors to either strengthen the selected hue or soften it.

☐ A monochromatic color scheme uses variations of a single color—for example, light blue, blue, and dark blue.

☐ A triadic color scheme pairs colors that are an equal distance from each other on the color wheel, such as red, yellow, and blue or orange, green, and purple.

□ A complementary color scheme uses color-wheel opposites such as red and green or orange and purple.

□ An analogous color scheme relies on adjacent colors on the color wheel, such as red, red-orange, and orange or blue, blue-green, and green.

Textural Dreams

Home decorating fabrics come in a variety of colors, textures, weights, weaves, and finishes. Each offers its own sense of style. Looking at magazines and home decorating books or visiting a home furnishings store are great ways to see what's current and how the experts have paired fabrics and accessories together successfully.

Here are just a few things to keep in mind when selecting a home decorator fabric. Most home decorator fabrics come in 54″ widths, unlike quilting or apparel fabrics, which typically come in narrower widths. This generous width is desirable to avoid piecing when upholstering furniture or creating window coverings, and it allows for the fabric to be "railroaded"—for example, a 50″-long curtain could have the fabric width as its length. "Railroading, "or running fabric horizontally, may save some of the yardage requirement. This time- and cost-saving technique works only with nondirectional fabrics. Fabrics that have a directional pattern or are napped—such as corduroy (a one-way directional pile)—are unsuitable for railroading.

Often napped fabrics, such as velveteen, require extra yardage, as all pieces have to be cut in the same direction for color consistency. To test for fabric nap, run your hand over the surface. If it feels smooth in one direction and rough in the other, the fabric has a nap. Napped fabric will also look darker when viewed from one direction.

Another distinguishing feature of most decorator fabrics is the need for dry cleaning. Special finishes, such as sizing or stain repellency, are often applied for easier care.

Listed below are some of the most commonly used decorator fabrics, along with their characteristics and suggested applications, but don't limit yourself—many wonderful fabrics are waiting to be found in quilting and garment fabric departments as well.

asian prints

These rich reds, golds, and royal blues with black accents work best with tailored lines. They can be paired with other silky fabrics, chenille, and touches of animal prints. Use these prints in smaller applications such as accessories, table-top fashions, pillows, and small chairs. Cotton Asian prints feel more casual than their shiny counterparts, creating a more informal look.

Asian prints

batiks

These resist-dyed fabrics offer a more relaxed influence and are perfect for pillows or table-top décor when used with canvas, duck, cotton, or denim.

Batiks are more casual.

brocades

Offering a rich formality with densely woven surface textures, these fabrics may be woven tone-on-tone, revealing the pattern in lighter or darker versions, or woven with two different colors for a more distinctive look. Think about pairing brocade with a lustrous stripe for a rich traditional look.

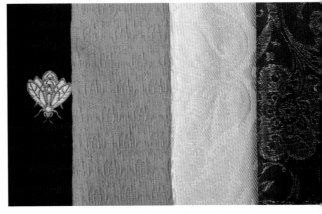

Brocades lend themselves to formality.

chenille

With its lush textures and color palettes, chenille adds warmth and a tactile dimension to furniture pieces, window treatments, throws, and pillows. This fabric is a bit of a chameleon, adapting readily to a variety of surroundings. Partner this sumptuous fabric with neutrals woven in geometric patterns for a contemporary look.

Chenille's lush textures

canvas, duck, and cotton twill

These casual fabrics all offer durability and a more casual feeling—great for kid- or animal-proofing any room. From large overstuffed furnishings to window treatments to pillows to the kitchen table, this fabric grouping has got it covered.

Canvas, duck, and twill

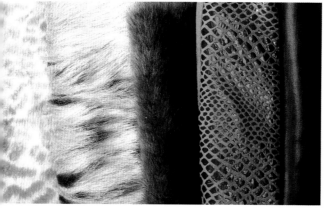

Make friends with the fauxs.

faux leathers, faux furs, and microsuedes

Offering the look of leather and suede at a fraction of the cost, these textures range from smooth to napped to delightfully embossed. This fabric group pairs with everything from traditional textures to eclectic, hip patterns but is best suited to tailored applications.

Florals and prints—a fabulous combination

floral cotton/poly prints

These fabrics are wonderfully versatile—from lightweight cotton for dish-towel trim to heavy cotton for duvets or elegant dining room drapes. Keep an eye on the scale of the print to fit the space and the project. Large-scale floral patterns need to be positioned where they will be the most pleasing—centered in furniture or on large-scale pillows and accessories. Smaller-scale prints are most effective on smaller pieces.

Check these out!

plaids and checks

Like their floral companions, these fabrics are limited only by their weight and scale. They can be comfortably casual at the breakfast table or classically chic in the dining room.

matelassé

Heavier weights of this soft, quilted-look double cloth are best used for coverlets, draperies, and upholstery and are a nice complement to stripes, florals, and toiles.

sheers

From window treatments to ethereal table runners to pillows, sachets, and shower curtains, these transparent fabrics suggest a delicate feel.

silks

Running the gamut from raw and rugged to light and luminous, and almost everything else in between, silks have become the new home-decorating staple. From window coverings to pillows and bedroom furnishings, this versatile fabric offers a rich texture and an elegant sheen that says glamour and quality. Look for remnants to incorporate into pillows or to trim the end of a table runner.

toiles

French traditional prints known for depicting seventeenth-century life, these single-color prints have become a decorating classic. They can be dressed up for a formal setting or can kick back when used with more durable fabrics such as heavy cottons and denims.

Special Themes

It's not uncommon to center a room's décor around a specific theme. Animals, sports, and hobbies are frequent choices. Used in moderation, a theme can unify a room.

The constant repetition of a single theme from walls to drapes to pillows and wastebaskets feels contrived. A more moderate approach, using the theme in either the walls or the curtains (not both) and then repeating it in pillows or an accessory, feels more balanced.

A mix of fabrics, colors, and textures all help create the room you love. Accessories can enhance not only the look of a room but its functionality. To create the perfect accent piece, look through the 15 projects presented here. It's a fast, fun, and easy way to accessorize your home. The trick is to start with an item that you love—be it a fabric piece, a theme, or a certain color. You can always find room for it!

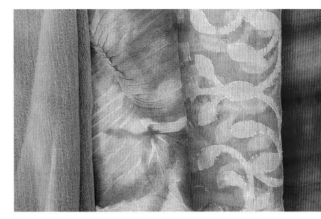

Light and delicate sheers

Sensational silk

Classic toile

the inside story

New accessories can totally change a room's look and feel. Adding a new, simple-to-sew pillow or fun desk accessory is a fast and easy way to provide an instant pick-me-up or accent that can give a room your personal touch.

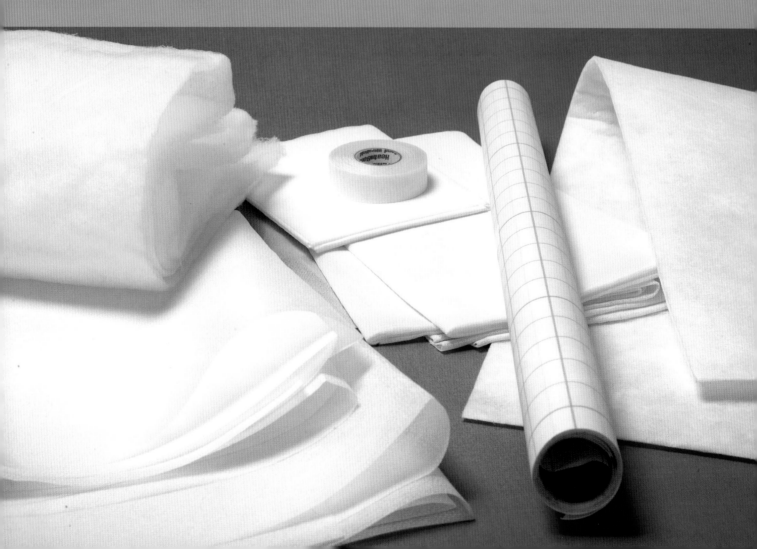

Choose your fabric and style, then get ready to gather the necessary inner components. But before you start gathering your materials, here's some important "inside" information.

What you put *in* your piece will affect its overall look and wear. Just because something isn't visible on the outside doesn't mean it's a place to cut corners.

The Stable, Supporting Cast

Like anything made by hand and with the heart, there are important components under the surface of the finished project—whether it's a blouse or a home décor item. When additional support is required, you will need to use nonwoven and fusible interfacings for your home décor projects. The successful home accessory needs just the right amount of firmness so it's stable without looking stiff. Take the time to test the selected fabric with a variety of interfacing weights to determine the proper level of support. For example, a set of everyday linen place mats that will be gently machine laundered calls for the added support of weft knit interfacing. This firmer interfacing provides just the right look and support for frequent use.

fun!

Start an interfacing sample set. As you test various fabrics with different interfacings, record the brands, weights, and types of interfacing on a 3″ × 5″ card. Attach your sample for easy reference when creating future projects.

Other types of stabilizers, such as tear- or wash-aways, provide localized reinforcement when you add decorative stitches or other machine embellishments to the fabric's surface. Positioning stabilizer directly under the fabric before stitching provides firmness exactly where it's needed, and the excess can be easily removed later.

Since many home décor projects call for additional firmness and shaping, look for a product that is multifunctional. One such timesaver, fast2fuse, is available in two weights. This stabilizer features a heat-activated adhesive on *both* sides, and adds both firmness and fusibility.

HeatnBond is a good choice when you want to adhere one fabric to another. This heat-sensitive webbing, which is available in narrow widths, sheets, or as yardage, is terrific for applying appliqués or fabrics to other fabrics and firm surfaces.

For kitchen and dining items that may be heat sensitive, consider using a heat-resistant nonwoven fleece such as Thermolam. Its properties slow the transfer of heat from one surface to another, offering a protective barrier. Additionally, it brings a nice loft to the finished project.

Take Care

Just as important as proper stabilization are the finished item's care requirements. Knowing in advance how the finished product will be cleaned determines what preparation is needed prior to sewing. For a set of washable cotton place mats, prewash all the fabrics and interfacing. A table runner made from home decorator fabric will most likely require dry cleaning, so prewashing isn't needed. When in doubt, test it out.

The Inside Stuff

After selecting the exterior fabric, the next important decision is the inside "stuffing." If you *expect* things to look good on the outside, put *good things* on the inside. Quality begets quality. Nothing can disappoint more than a fabulous project that doesn't hold up due to poor-quality insides.

Batting, foam, and fiber fill

resilient foam

Foam slabs are great for pillows and cushion inserts. Adding these spongy pads can readily change or alter the look of a sofa, bed, or chair. Foam comes in a variety of densities and premade shapes, and it can be purchased precut or easily cut to a specific shape using an electric knife. Projects such as pillows and bolsters call for standard, light-density foam pillow forms, not meant to bear much weight. For durable seat cushions, look for denser foams made for firmer support.

somewhat batty

Batting is what puts the *"cush"* in cushioning. Because of their versatility, both batting and its loose counterpart, fiberfill, have multiple uses in home décor projects—from potholders to pillows and from quilts to dream boards.

Batting can be made from cotton, polyester, silk, wool, or a mix of these fibers. It comes in a variety of thicknesses and is available by the yard or in prepackaged sizes. The added fluff of batting increases yardage requirements, so be sure to allow for loft take-up.

Loose polyester fiberfill is great for stuffing those hard-to-reach areas such as pillow corners and tiny spaces.

easy!

For a comfortable, cushiony surface, wrap the foam form in a layer of polyester batting.

fast!

To stuff wimpy pillow corners, wrap polyester fiberfill around one end of a chopstick or a fondue fork, then carefully push it into place. With your outside hand, pinch the newly positioned batting and hold it in place while you carefully retract your other hand from inside the project.

Perfect Piping or Wonderful Welting

In home décor sewing, the terms welting and piping are used interchangeably. Here's a list of what welting or piping can do.

☐ Strengthen seams (add it first to the half that requires the most control)

☐ Define a shape (be sure to add it to all seams for consistency)

☐ Add subtlety with a small, fine cord or a dramatic effect with a large cord

☐ Add surface interest by introducing a new texture to the mix

☐ Provide diversion if adjoining fabrics aren't lining up just right

☐ Produce professional-looking results

Welting is made from thick cotton string or cable cord ranging from ⅛″ to 2″ in diameter. Premade welting is offered in a variety of sizes and colors, but if the color or size available isn't what you'd envisioned, it's easy to make your own. Whether matching the fabric or introducing a coordinating print or a bold contrast color, you can create the size and look that's just right for your project.

Piping accents the journal tab.

easy!

To minimize bulk from frequent piecing, plan to purchase extra yardage for custom welting. A half-yard of 45″-wide fabric will yield bias strips approximately 24″ long.

make your own welting

1. Start with bias fabric strips cut at a 45° angle to the selvage; these provide optimal flexibility and are easy to use around corners.

2. Measure the circumference of the cord and add *double* the desired seam allowance. Also add an extra ⅜″ to the total for a sewing allowance.

Example: ¾″ cording circumference

+ 1″ (½″ seam allowance × 2)

+ ⅜″ (for sewing ease)

2⅛″ total strip width needed

3. Measure the total length needed, plus 3″, to determine how many bias strips to cut.

4. Piece the fabric strips to the desired length, using a diagonal seam. Trim to ¼″, then press the seams open.

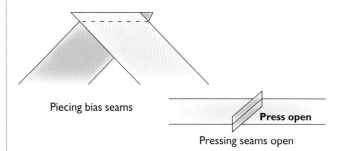

Piecing bias seams

Press open

Pressing seams open

5. Place the welting in the center of the wrong side of the fabric strip and fold the strip in half, encasing it. Match the long cut edges of the strip and pin in place.

6. Use a piping, cording, or zipper foot and sew as close to the welt as possible. Change the needle position on your machine to stitch even closer if the foot allows it.

fast!

If you plan to do several home décor projects, purchase a piping or cording foot—it provides a closer and cleaner stitching line than the standard zipper foot.

It is truly gratifying when the items you've made really pull together a room's new look. The time and effort spent selecting the best fabrics and inside components really do provide long-term benefits.

effortless embellishments

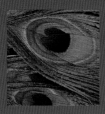

Details make a difference—especially when it comes to home décor. The simple addition of trims such as piping, tassels, beads, or feathers transforms something plain into something **dynamic.**

Trims enhance and draw attention wherever they're applied, and they're so *easy* to do. Inserted into a seam or attached to the surface, trims can be machine sewn, hand sewn, fused, or glued. With the vast trim assortment offered today, the only challenge is deciding which one is best suited to your project—and who says you can use only one?

fun!

Gather your favorite magazine clippings, fabrics, and trims. Lay them out together for a while to let your eye adapt to the new look and see what inspiration bubbles up.

Tantalizing Trims

Here are just a few reasons to give these terrific trims a try:

- Trims add instant color and texture.

- They can marry two unrelated fabrics and make them look irresistible.

- Trims offer an optical illusion by creating a focal point or diverting the eye.

- Trims can camouflage a sewing mishap or disguise a fabric shortage.

- They can vary in prominence depending on the need—as subtle and delicate as baby rickrack or as large and substantial as a double band of beaded tassels.

easy!

Many trims unravel once cut. Be sure to tape each end *prior* to cutting. Remove the tape after the end has been secured.

Just as your fabric selection dictates a certain look, so does the choice of trims. Following are a few of the types of embellishments available.

Gimp is a flat braid or trim without an edge or lip. Lipped trims are often referred to as pipings. Piping needs to be sewn into a seam or added to a folded edge; gimp or flat braid may be machine applied to the surface or at an edge.

Braid, gimp, and pom-poms, oh my!

Fringe comes in a variety of lengths and textures. It ranges from straight and very delicate, to long and luxurious, to wild and wacky. Cut fringe shows a lot of movement. Looped fringe offers more texture and bulk. Either type can be applied at the project edge or on the surface, wherever extra attention is desired.

Fringe benefits

Bullion refers to lush, long, twisted ropelike fringe. It creates an opulent, weighty feel. Apply it with two rows of stitching at or near the project edge for some much-needed stabilization.

easy!

Add bullion fringe or tassels on the edges of a pillow for added interest.

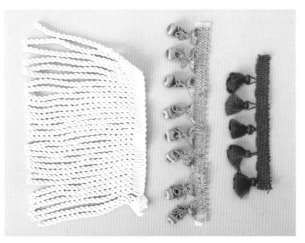

Opulent touches with bullion and fringe

Tassels range in size from petite and demure to large and dense. They can be purchased individually or as a length of trim. This fun detail offers a rich touch. When purchasing tasseled trim, take a moment to examine each tassel to ensure that it is well constructed. Nothing is more disheartening than bringing home the trim to find a tassel missing or falling apart.

Using a tassel is like adding an exclamation point!

fun!

Try your hand at creating a custom tassel using embroidery floss, yarn, or ribbon.

Creating your own tassels is as easy as 1, 2, 3. You can mix and match yarns, ribbons, or even bead strands to your heart's content.

There are lots of tassel-making tools available, but one of the simplest is a piece of cardboard or a 3″ × 5″ card.

1. Determine the tassel's desired length and cut a piece of cardboard to match. Cut 2 lengths of yarn. Lay the first horizontally across the cardboard's upper edge to form a hang cord. Wrap the tassel yarns vertically until the desired fullness is reached.

2. At the upper edge, tie the hang cord around the wrapped yarns. At the lower edge, cut the tassel yarns.

3. Wrap the second yarn length tightly around the cut yarns to form a neck. Trim the tassel evenly. Tie a second knot at the hanger's ends.

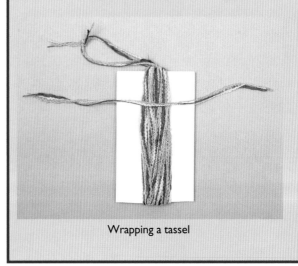

Wrapping a tassel

easy!

Pull two unrelated colors together with coordinating ribbons.

Don't let a fabric or trim shortage stop you cold. Look at it as a creative opportunity. Stand back and ask, what else could this piece use?

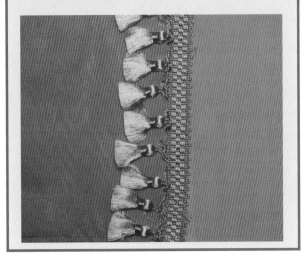

fabulous feathers

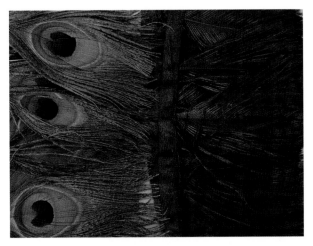

Feather your nest.

Seeking something exotic? Why not "feather" your own nest? Feathers add a three-dimensional quality. Their presence suggests whimsy, abundance, and

luxury, so care needs to be taken when applying feather trim.

Keep the feathers at a 90° angle when sewing them on. This allows your needle to secure the feathers easily and maintains a clean look to the project. Feather trim has a ribbon edge to ease the application process. What do you do if your feathers are ruffled and fall off? Not to worry—a spot of craft glue will keep you and your project intact.

bodacious beads

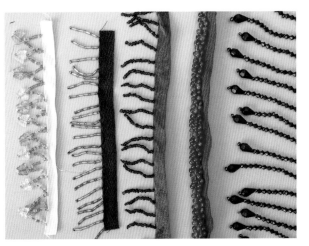

Make a bead-dazzling statement.

From rustic and earthy to glittery and glamorous, beaded trims abound. They run the gamut from a simple beaded row or two to very detailed ornate strands. Some beaded trims come with a lip that requires an in-seam application; others may be applied directly to the project edge or surface.

When selecting a beaded trim, consider the bead's makeup. Beads can be glass or plastic and each type has its own inherent characteristics. Glass beads offer the best quality and luster, but they're also heavy. Heavier beads require additional stabilization to support the weight. Plastic beads are generally less lustrous, more durable, and less weighty, making them easier to apply and long lasting for everyday use. Plastic beads are best cleaned by hand, as dry cleaning chemicals will alter the beads' appearance.

Still can't find exactly what you're looking for? Make your own unique trims! Consider mixing and matching a variety of trims. If a color can't be closely matched, use a contrasting welting, fringe, or gathered ruffle.

fun!

Make your own contrasting trim from triangular fabric pieces. Sew the two angled sides right sides together. Turn and press, then overlap the triangles along the seam edge, matching the raw edges.

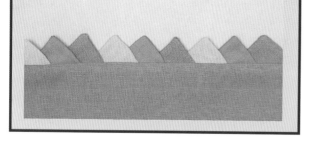

The Proper Care and Feeding of Trims

Select durable trims, particularly for high-use items. Prior to construction, when appropriate, preshrink the trim along with the fashion fabric. Delicate trims may require dry cleaning and should be used in low-wear areas.

Whether you opt for just a touch of texture, such as a braided gimp, or go for all-out opulence with a dense, elaborate fringe, be aware that each embellishment adds more depth and visual weight to its intended piece. For subtlety, keep your trim selection to matching colors, narrow widths, and uncomplicated styles. Conversely, for sophistication, opt for trims that offer color, texture, and design contrast. And if one trim isn't enough, consider adding more until the desired level of embellishment is achieved.

Whatever your preference, know this: embellishment is eye candy! It provides tactile relief for the sensory-deprived. So get out and start playing. A word of caution... beautiful, fun trims are addictive—once you start using and collecting them, it's very hard to stop!

at
your desk

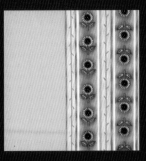
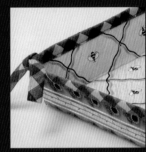

No-Sew Desk Blotter

FINISHED SIZE: 18″ × 24″

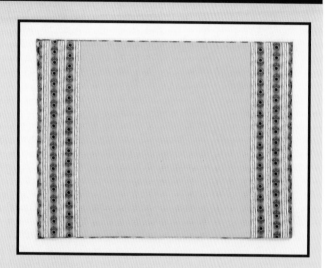

Blot out boring seat time at your desk with this fast and fun no-sew desk blotter. It's a clever way to put together a polished, personalized desk set. Combine with any or all of the other fun desk accessories and you have a desk made in heaven.

What You'll Need

- □ 20″ × 30″ × ³⁄₁₆″ foam-core board
- □ ⅝ yard 36″-wide gold felt
- □ 1 yard 45″-wide blue-and-gold check fabric
- □ ¾ yard blue coordinate
- □ ⅝ yard heavyweight fast2fuse
- □ Fabric or craft glue
- □ Craft knife
- □ Rotary cutter, ruler, and mat

How Tos

cutting

Prewash and press the fabric before cutting.

1. Cut 1 rectangle 21″ × 24″ of the gold felt for the blotter front.

2. Cut 1 bias rectangle 23″ × 29″ of the blue-and-gold check for the blotter back.

3. Cut 2 rectangles 12″ × 22″ of the blue coordinate for the side pockets.

4. Trim the foam-core board to 18″ × 24″.

5. Cut 1 rectangle 17¾″ × 23¾″ of the heavyweight fast2fuse.

assembly

1. Press the felt flat. With wrong sides together, center the fast2fuse on it, leaving a 1½″ border at the upper and lower edges; keep the side edges even.

2. Turn the blotter over and fuse the the felt border pieces to the back side.

easy!

Because of the felt's density, allow additional fusing time.

3. Fold the pocket in half lengthwise, with wrong sides together. Press along the fold.

4. With the blotter right side up, center the pocket fold 4″ from the front side edge of the blotter. Pin in place.

5. Fold the lower and upper edges of the pocket to the wrong side of the blotter; fuse in place.

6. Fold the long edge of the pocket to the wrong side and fuse in place.

Fold the raw edges.

7. Place the bias-cut backing wrong side up. Center the foam board, leaving a 2½" fabric border.

8. Turn the upper border of the backing down and glue it in place, smoothing the fabric with your hand.

9. Repeat for the lower border, pulling the fabric taut for a firm fit.

10. Tuck in the corners and fold the side edges to the wrong side and glue in place.

11. Center the front blotter on top of the back blotter, covering the glued edges.

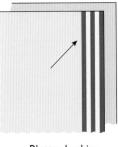

Blotter backing

12. Apply a liberal amount of glue to the exposed board and fabric edges. With your hand, firmly press the front into position. Allow the glue to dry.

Hold Everything Desk Tray

FINISHED SIZE: 9″ × 13″ × 2″

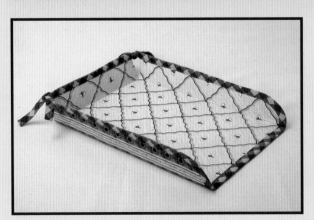

Here's the perfect place to stash those loose assorted papers that you might need soon or will wait until later to file.

What You'll Need

- ½ yard each of three different fabrics (A, B, C)
- ½ yard heavyweight fast2fuse
- Matching thread
- Air-soluble fabric marker
- Nonstick pressing sheet
- See-through ruler
- ⅜″-wide HeatnBond UltraHold iron-on adhesive (optional)
- Rotary cutter, ruler, and mat

How Tos

cutting

Prewash and press the fabric before cutting.

1. Enlarge the pattern on next page, and use it to cut one piece each of fabrics A and B; add ½˝ to all outside edges.

2. Using the pattern provided, cut one fast2fuse tray. Trim an additional ⅛˝ at the upper notched areas.

3. Cut 2˝-wide strips of bias trim from fabric C and piece with diagonal seams until the strip totals 60˝.

assembly

Note: All seam allowances are ½˝, unless otherwise stated.

1. With right sides together, pin the notched edges of tray fabric A to fabric B. Stitch a ½˝ seam. Clip a diagonal line to the inner corner. Trim the seam allowance to ¼˝.

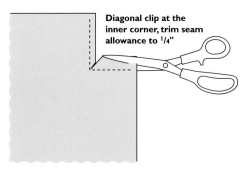

Diagonal clip at the inner corner, trim seam allowance to ¹/₄"

Prepare tray for fast2fuse.

2. Press the seams open. Turn the tray right side out and press the corners. Turn wrong side out again.

3. Following the manufacturer's instructions, fuse the fast2fuse stiffener to the wrong side of one fabric tray, placing the notched area just below the stitching line.

4. Turn the tray right side out and fuse the second side.

5. Using the see-through ruler and an air-soluble fabric marker, draw a straight horizontal line across the back of the tray between the 2 notched edges.

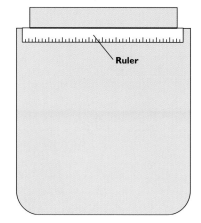

Ruler

Draw a straight line between the notches.

6. Draw 2 vertical lines 9˝ apart by aligning the ruler vertically with the upper notched edge.

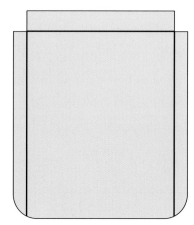

Draw fold lines.

7. With matching thread, stitch along the drawn lines.

8. Fold the tray back on all stitched lines and press to form a crease.

9. Trim the excess fabric from the fast2fuse edges on top, bottom, and sides.

10. Press the raw edges of the bias trim under ½″ on one long side and both short ends. Fold the trim in half lengthwise, enclosing the edges. Press.

11. Open one edge of the bias trim. Fold in short ends ¼″. Leaving a 4½″ end of trim unattached at the notched corner, pin the trim to the tray's outer side, right sides together. Pin from one side around the curved bottom and to the other sides, leaving 4½″ at the top corner, then cutting the trim. Using a ⅜″ seam allowance, stitch the bias strip. Attach the remaining trim across the top edge of the tray, leaving 4½″ extra at each end.

12. Wrap the folded bias strip over the raw edges of the tray, enclosing them. Stitch the binding in place and continue stitching the ends of the strips together to create ties. Tie the trim ends together to form the corners of the tray.

fast!

Instead of stitching the bias trim, fuse the trim to the seam allowances with HeatnBond UltraHold iron-on adhesive.

Variation

Change the dimensions slightly and tie up all 4 corners, and you'll have a bread tray that matches the pieces in the On the Patio section.

Simple adjustments change the tray to a dining accessory.

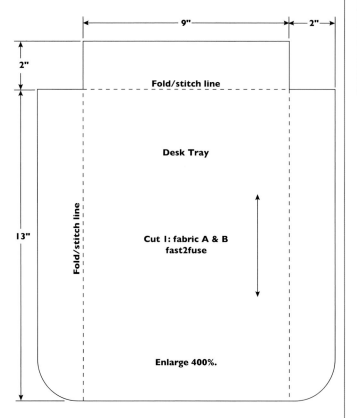

9″ · 2″

2″

Fold/stitch line

13″

Fold/stitch line

Desk Tray

**Cut 1: fabric A & B
fast2fuse**

Enlarge 400%.

Ah-choo! Tissue Box Cover

FINISHED SIZE: 4½″ × 4½″ × 5″

This perfect add-on accessory with its own slipcover will be welcome in any room of the house—and you just might forget that it's as functional as it is pretty.

What You'll Need

- Scrap at least 5″ × 15″ (fabric A)
- ¾ yard of 45″-wide blue-and-gold check (fabric B)
- Scrap at least 5″ × 15″ (fabric C)
- ⅓ yard heavyweight fast2fuse
- 12″ yellow yarn
- Two ⅝″ yellow buttons
- Matching thread
- Basic sewing supplies
- Air-soluble marker
- Square box of tissues
- Rotary cutter, ruler, and mat

How Tos

cutting

Prewash and press the fabric before cutting.

1. Cut 1 rectangle 4½″ × 15″ of fabric A for the cover.

2. Cut 1 rectangle 4½″ × 15″ of fabric C for the lining.

3. Cut 4 rectangles 4¼″ × 5″ of fast2fuse.

4. Cut 1 square 4¼″ × 4¼″ of fast2fuse.

5. Cut 1 square 15¾″ × 15¾″ of fabric B.

assembly

Note: All seam allowances are ½″ unless otherwise stated.

1. Fold under ½″ on all sides of the fabric B square. Topstitch in place. Lay the square flat and mark its center.

2. Place the 4¼″ × 4¼″ fast2fuse square in the center of the *right* side of the square fabric. Fuse following the manufacturer's instructions. Leaving a ¼″ gap, place 2 fast2fuse rectangles on each side of the center square and fuse in place.

Center the fast2fuse.

3. Fold under ¼″ on the sides of the cover rectangle fabric A and press. Fuse to the fast2 fuse.

Center the rectangle on the square.

4. Turn the fabric square over to the wrong side and position the remaining fast2fuse rectangles above and below the center, leaving a ¼″ gap. Fuse in place.

Position fast2fuse on wrong side.

5. Fold under ¼″ on the sides of the lining rectangle fabric C and press. With the fast2fuse side up, place the lining right side up and fuse in place.

6. With an air-soluble marker, trace a tissue opening on the right side of the top of the cover. Machine baste around the traced line. Cut out the oval on the inside of the basted line.

7. Position the yellow yarn around the edge of the opening between the stitching and cut edge. With matching thread, satin stitch (a very tight zigzag stitch) over the yarn and edge twice.

8. Place the cover over a tissue box.

9. Fold the loose fabric to form a triangle across the yellow side. Repeat on the other side, overlapping the previous fold. Hand stitch the corner in place.

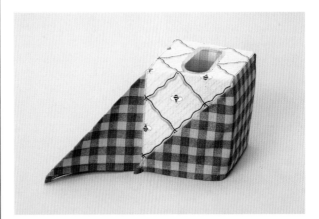

Intersecting folds

10. Add a button ½″ below the intersecting folds. Repeat for the opposite side.

Capture the Moment Photo Frame

FINISHED SIZE: 6¾″ × 10½″

Here's a fast, fun, and easy way to personalize any photo or card that holds special meaning.

This frame accommodates a 4″ × 6″ photo.

What You'll Need

- ⅜ yard fabric A
- ⅜ yard fabric B
- ⅓ yard fabric C
- ⅜ yard fast2fuse
- ⅜ yard heavyweight fast2fuse
- 5″ × 7″ lightweight muslin scrap
- Spray adhesive
- 4 buttons (⅜″ coverable half-ball)
- ¾ yard ½″-wide HeatnBond UltraHold iron-on adhesive
- Nonstick pressing sheet
- Matching thread
- Air-soluble fabric marker
- Rotary cutter, ruler, and mat
- Seam sealant
- 12″ see-through ruler
- One 4″ × 6″ photo or card

How Tos

cutting

Prewash and press the fabric before cutting. Use the pattern on page 28 to cut your pieces.

1. Cut 1 photo frame front from fabric A, adding 1″ to all the sides.

2. Cut 1 frame front lining from fabric B.

3. Cut 1 frame back from fabric C.

4. Cut a 5″ × 7″ rectangle from muslin.

5. Cut 1 frame each from regular and heavy-weight fast2fuse.

6. Cut 4 button circles from fabric B.

assembly

1. Following the manufacturer's instructions, fuse the photo frame front and front lining to opposite sides of the regular fast2fuse.

2. Locate the center of the frame by measuring $4\frac{3}{8}''$ from the bottom edge and $3\frac{3}{8}''$ from the side edge.

3. Transfer the corner dots on the pattern to the lining of the frame.

4. Using a straightedge and the fabric marker, draw $6\frac{3}{4}''$-long diagonal lines from one corner dot to the other, through the center, to form an X.

5. Use a rotary cutter to cut along the lines to create flaps. Add a dot of seam sealant to each corner. Allow to dry.

Cut an X to release the frame.

6. Using matching thread, satin stitch all the edges, pivoting at the dots.

7. Position the muslin where the photo will be placed on one side of the heavyweight fast2fuse. Fuse in place.

8. Place the selected photo right side up on the muslin.

easy!

Use the top frame to double-check the photo placement.

9. Use a spray adhesive to adhere the photo to the desired position on the muslin.

10. Place the muslin, photo side down to the wrong side of the frame front, sandwiching the photo. Keeping the front fabric edges free, fuse the muslin edges to the wrong side of the frame front, using a dry iron and nonstick pressing sheet.

11. Fold the front fabric edges to the photo back, covering all raw fast2fuse edges and fuse in place. Repeat for the upper and lower edges, folding the excess fabric in place.

12. Turn the frame back fabric under $\frac{1}{2}''$ and press in place.

13. With the back of the photo facing up, center the back fabric over the exposed fabric edges and apply strips of HeatnBond along each edge.

fast!

Fuse any loose backing edge in place with small strips of HeatnBond UltraHold iron-on adhesive.

14. Cover the half-ball buttons.

15. On the right side of the frame, turn back each flap to reveal the photo and tack to the frame.

16. Sew a button at the point of each flap, catching the top fabric of the frame to secure.

Variation

Here's a great idea: why not create a travel-size photo frame that sports two small photos? It's a perfect way to keep your favorite moments with you...at the office, in the car, or on the go.

Travel frame for those on the go

Enlarge 400%.

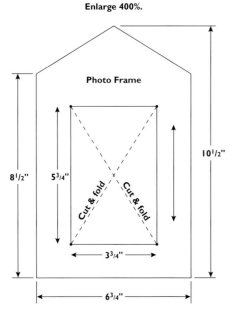

Photo Frame

10¹/₂"

8¹/₂"

5³/₄"

Cut & fold

Cut & fold

3³/₄"

6³/₄"

**Cut 1: Fabric A, B, & C,
regular fast2fuse,
heavyweight fast2fuse**

Waste Not, Want Not Basket

FINISHED SIZE: 10″ × 7″ × 10″

Who says that trash can't make a fashion statement? Here's one wastepaper basket that advances its service to more than collecting trash. This is the perfect way to make the basket the ideal accessory in any room of the house.

What You'll Need

- One self-adhesive wastepaper basket
- 1 yard 45″–60″-wide fabric
- 1 yard looped trim
- 2 yards rickrack trim
- Air-soluble marker
- Fabric glue

How Tos

cutting

Prewash and press the fabric before cutting.

Use the wastepaper basket's label to trace and cut 1 cover.

fast!

What could be easier than a peel-n-stick surface? Allow a little extra length, as bias fabric tends to stretch, taking up some length.

assembly

1. Press under ¼″ on one short end of the cover.

2. Preplan your starting and ending point at one edge of the wastebasket.

3. Stick the cover onto the basket, applying the pressed edge last to overlap the starting edge.

4. Glue the pressed edge in place, folding under the raw edge.

5. Apply a bead of glue to the basket's uppermost edge. Press the looped fringe into place, aligning the starting point of the fringe with the cover's starting point.

6. Add a second layer of glue to the middle of the fringe's header. Press the rickrack trim into place. Fold the raw edge under.

7. Apply a final row of glue to the lower edge and press the rickrack into place.

easy!

For a richer trim, layer a length of coordinating ribbon under the rickrack.

Variation

Got a sports fan in your house? Here's a quick way to put some sporting action into gear. Talk about a clean shot! Who could resist a little 2-point action, all in the name of a clean room?

Score some points for this basket!

on the
patio

Table-top Fashions Times Two

FINISHED SIZE: 14″ × 70″

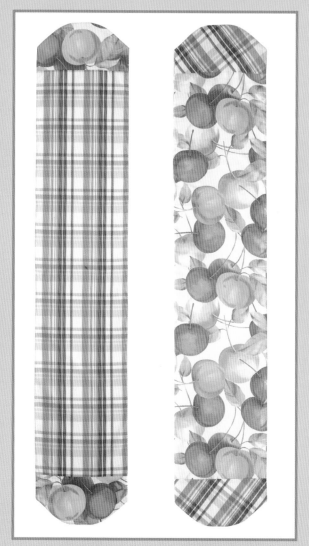

For the same amount of time it takes to make one runner, you can have two by making it reversible! Nothing could be cheerier than this delightful table runner—so why not double your enjoyment?

fast!

Use two coordinating fabrics for easy table-top mixing and matching. It doubles the look and wear for the same sewing and laundering time.

What You'll Need

- ☐ 1¾ yards *each* fabric A and B
- ☐ 2 yards Thermolam (or a heat-resistant nonwoven fleece interfacing)
- ☐ Matching thread
- ☐ Pinking shears (optional)
- ☐ 6″ length of ½″-wide HeatnBond UltraHold iron-on adhesive
- ☐ Rotary cutter, ruler, and mat

easy!

When making items for the kitchen or dining room, add a heat-resistant interfacing to protect your dining surfaces.

How Tos

cutting

Prewash and press the fabric before cutting.

1. Fabric A: Cut 1 center section 15″ × 58″.

Cut 2 curved ends 15″ × 7¼″, using the pattern on page 35.

2. Fabric B: Cut 1 center section 15″ × 58″.

Cut 2 bias curved ends 15″ × 7¼″, using the pattern on page 35.

3. Thermolam: Cut 1 rectangle 15″ × 72″.

4. HeatnBond iron-on adhesive: Cut one 5″ length.

assembly

Note: All seam allowances are ½″, unless otherwise stated.

1. With right sides together, pin the short edge of the center section (fabric B) to the table runner end piece (fabric A). Stitch and press the seam open. Trim the seam allowance to ¼″.

2. Repeat for the second end.

3. Make a second table runner from the opposite fabrics, following Steps 1 and 2.

4. Place the Thermolam insert on the wrong side of 1 table runner. Pin in place.

5. With right sides together, pin the runners together. Stitch around the runners, catching the Thermolam in the stitching; leave a 5″ opening for turning.

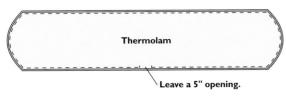

Stitch around the runner.

6. Trim the straight seam allowances to ¼″. Pink the curved edges to ¼″ or clip the seam allowance on the curves.

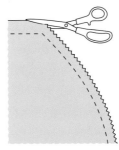

Trim edges before turning.

7. Reach through the opening and turn the table runner right side out. Turn the seam allowance inside and press the runner flat.

8. Fuse the opening closed using the HeatnBond.

fun!

Make a couple of table runners to use in lieu of place mats. Simply position them at the table where you would use a place mat.

Pretty and Practical Place Mats

FINISHED SIZE: 14˝ × 19˝

Take two great fabrics, add a solid insulation, and you have the makings of a double dose of pleasing place mats.

What You'll Need

Note: Yardage is for a set of 4 reversible place mats.

- ☐ 1½ yards each 45˝-wide fabric A and fabric B
- ☐ 2 yards Thermolam (or a heat-resistant nonwoven fleece interfacing)
- ☐ Matching thread
- ☐ 12˝ length of ½˝-wide HeatnBond UltraHold iron-on adhesive
- ☐ Pinking shears (optional)
- ☐ Rotary cutter, ruler, and mat

How Tos

cutting

Use the pattern on page 35 for the end pieces.

Prewash and press the fabric before cutting.

1. Cut 4 rectangles 11½˝ × 15˝ each from fabric A and fabric B.

2. Cut 8 ends each from fabric A and fabric B.

assembly

Note: All seam allowances are ½˝, unless otherwise stated.

1. With right sides together, pin the straight edge of the end of the place mat (fabric B) to the long edge of fabric A.

2. Stitch and press the seam open. Trim the seam allowance to ¼˝.

3. Repeat for the second end.

4. Make a second place mat front from the opposite fabrics, following Steps 1–3.

5. Using the finished mat front for a pattern, cut 4 inserts of Thermolam.

6. Place a Thermolam insert on the wrong side of one place mat front. Pin in place.

7. With right sides together, pin the place mat fronts together. Stitch around the place mat, catching the Thermolam in the stitching. Leave a 3″ opening for turning.

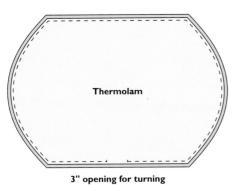

Thermolam

3" opening for turning

Catch the Thermolam in the stitching.

8. Trim the straight seam allowances to ¼″. Pink the curved edges to ¼″, or clip the seam allowances.

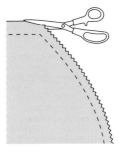

Trim edges before turning.

9. Reach through the opening and turn the place mat right side out. Press the place mat flat.

10. Insert a 3″ strip of HeatnBond UltraHold into the opening and fuse closed.

11. Repeat Steps 1–10 for the remaining place mats.

All-Occasion Napkins

FINISHED SIZE: 14″ × 14″

Napkins made from 100% cotton are the perfect choice. They are soft to the touch, absorbent, and launder easily. Sewing two pieces of fabric of comparable weight together makes them reversible.

What You'll Need

Note: Yardage is for 4 napkins.

☐ 1 yard each of fabric A and B

☐ Matching thread

☐ Rotary cutter and mat

How Tos

cutting

1. Cut 4 squares 15″ × 15″ from fabric A.

2. Cut 4 squares 15″ × 15″ from fabric B.

sewing the napkin

Note: All seam allowances are ½″, unless otherwise stated.

Prewash and press the fabric before cutting.

1. For a reversible napkin, place fabric A right sides together with fabric B. Pin around all 4 edges, leaving a 2″ opening on 1 side.

2. Stitch around all 4 sides, leaving a 2″ opening for turning.

3. Clip the corners. Trim the seam allowance to ¼″.

4. Reach through the opening and turn the napkin right side out.

5. Tuck under the opening edges and hand stitch or fuse closed.

fun!

For added embellishment, consider topstitching or adding some washable trim such as ribbon, fringe, rickrack, contrasting seam binding, or embroidery.

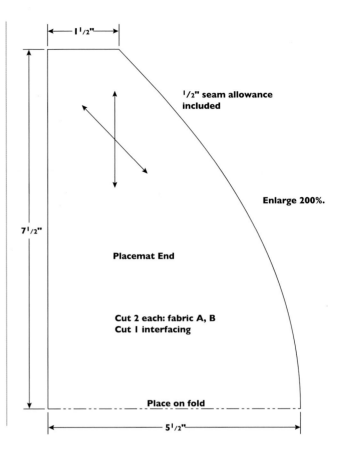

1½"

7½"

½" seam allowance included

Enlarge 200%.

Placemat End

Cut 2 each: fabric A, B
Cut 1 interfacing

Place on fold

5½"

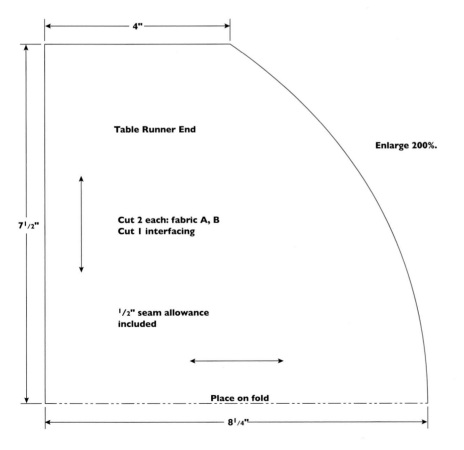

4"

Table Runner End

7½"

Cut 2 each: fabric A, B
Cut 1 interfacing

½" seam allowance included

Enlarge 200%.

Place on fold

8¼"

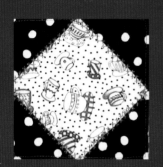

kitchen
treats

Cooking Up Fun Apron

FINISHED SIZE: 25″ × 28½″

Serve up some sewing fun with this very *functional* apron. Suitable for cooks of all kinds, this easy-to-sew apron features dish-towel fabric and quilt binding and can be whipped up in no time. With rave reviews expected, be prepared to serve up a second helping.

What You'll Need

- ⅞ yard 45″-wide terry-cloth fabric
- 6 yards quilt binding in a coordinating color
- ¼ yard cotton coordinating fabric
- Matching thread
- Fabric marker
- Rotary cutter, ruler, and mat

How Tos

cutting

Prewash and press the fabric before cutting.

1. Cut a rectangle 25″ wide × 30″ long from the terry-cloth fabric.

2. Fold the cut fabric in half the long way. Make a mark along the short edge 6″ from the upper cut corner. Place another mark 10″ from the corner along the long edge. Place 4 additional marks at 2″ vertical intervals from the top: 5¾″ from the outside edge, 5″ from the edge, 4″ from the edge, and 2½″ from the edge. Draw a slightly curved line connecting the marks from the top edge to the side edge.

3. Cut along the line, creating the front curved edges of the apron.

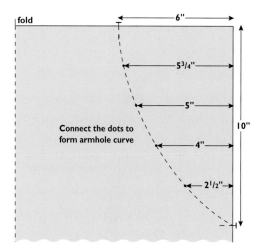

fold

6"

5³/₄"

5"

10"

4"

2¹/₂"

Connect the dots to form armhole curve

Apron shaping cut from a rectangle

4. Cut a rectangle 9½″ × 14″ from the coordinating pocket fabric.

5. From the bias binding cut 2 strips 20″ long and 2 strips 84″ long.

assembly

Note: All seam allowances are ½″, unless otherwise stated.

1. Use an overcast stitch, zigzag stitch, or serge to finish the apron's upper and lower edges.

2. Turn under 1″ to the wrong side of the apron's upper and lower edges. Press and topstitch in place ¾″ from the folded edge.

3. With right sides together, fold the pocket rectangle crosswise to measure 7″ × 9½″.

4. Stitch around the pocket's 3 sides, leaving a 2″ opening for turning. Clip across the corners. Turn the pocket right side out and tuck in the opening. Press.

5. Center the pocket 8″ from the side edges and 7¼″ from the lower edge. Pin and stitch side and bottom edges.

6. Open one end of the shorter binding strip and fold in ½″. Press and refold. Stitch around the sides and bottom.

7. Position the folded edge at the apron's lower side edge. Place the fabric edge in the middle of the binding. Pin the binding over the side raw edge, encasing it. Topstitch the binding in place. Repeat on the other side.

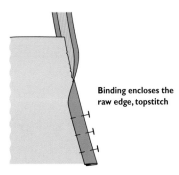

Binding encloses the raw edge, topstitch

Pin the binding.

8. Open each end of the remaining binding strips and fold in ½″. Press and refold.

9. Measure in 20″ from the end of one strip and place a pin. Begin pinning the binding to the apron's upper edge at the 20″ mark. Continue pinning along the curved side, encasing the raw edge as before. Pin the remaining binding together with the folded edges meeting. Topstitch along the binding's entire length. Repeat for the other side.

10. The apron knots at the neck and double ties at the waist.

Variation

Artiste/chef's assistant apron

Important works of art are no small endeavors—especially when generated from the heart of a child. Whether the child is a budding artiste or a designated chef's assistant, this fun vinyl apron will make cleanup a breeze. Surprise your favorite child with this artful rendition that's just plain, doggone fun.

Almost any fabric can be made child-proof with the welcomed addition of iron-on vinyl. Always use a press cloth or Teflon iron sole to prevent melting the vinyl.

easy!

To achieve the desired width, the vinyl may be pieced by butting one raw edge against the other. Turn the garment over and press from the wrong side.

A Dish Towel With a Past

FINISHED SIZE: 17½″ × 26″

Complete with a ribbon hanger, this towel will bring joy to any kitchen and its activities. With this fun retro print, this towel does more than take a fast pass at the dishes.

What You'll Need

- ☐ ⅞ yard 17½″-wide dish-towel fabric
- ☐ ⅜ yard 36″- or 45″-wide print fabric
- ☐ 1⅛ yard rickrack
- ☐ ⅙ yard ⅝″-wide ribbon
- ☐ Scrap 6″ × 6″ of second coordinating fabric
- ☐ 6″ × 6″ of HeatnBond UltraHold iron-on adhesive
- ☐ Matching thread
- ☐ Rotary cutter, ruler, and mat

How Tos

cutting

Prewash and press the fabric before cutting.

1. Cut 1 rectangle 17½″ × 27″ from the dish-towel fabric.

2. Cut 1 rectangle band 9″ × 19″ from the coordinating print fabric.

3. Cut one motif 3″ × 3″ from the print fabric.

4. Cut one 4″ length of ribbon.

5. Cut 1 square 6″ × 6″ of the second coordinating fabric scrap.

6. Cut 1 scrap 6″ × 6″ of HeatnBond UltraHold iron-on adhesive.

7. Cut 2 lengths 19″ long of rickrack.

assembly

Note: All seam allowances are ½″ unless otherwise stated.

1. Turn under ¼″ at the towel's upper edge. Press. Turn again ¼″; press.

2. Trim one end of the ribbon at an angle. Place the angled edge 2″ from the corner into the pressed hem. Topstitch across the upper edge of the towel, stitching the ribbon in place.

3. Position the ribbon's loose end at a diagonal at the towel's long side, 2″ from the corner. Tuck the end under to align with the side and stitch across the ribbon to secure it.

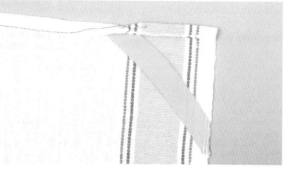

Add a handy hanger.

4. Press the large band's sides under ½″.

5. Align the band and sides of the towel. Pin the right side of the band to the towel's wrong side at the lower edge with raw edges even. Use a 1″ seam allowance to stitch together. Press the seam toward the band.

6. Fold under ½″ at the band's top edge and press.

7. Fold the band to the towel's front side, enclosing the raw edges, and pin in place. Baste the band's top edge in place, 6″ from the lower edge.

easy!

Fuse the sides of the band and toweling together with small strips of HeatnBond UltraHold iron-on adhesive.

8. Center one rickrack strip over the band's edge. Fold rickrack ends to the wrong side. Pin in place and stitch. Repeat for the towel's lower edge.

9. Following the manufacturer's instructions, press the HeatnBond iron-on adhesive square to the wrong side of the coordinate's motif.

10. Fold under ¼″ on all 4 sides. Center the motif to the right side of the 6″ × 6″ coordinate. Pin in place and fuse.

11. Apply a row of decorative appliqué stitches around the motif.

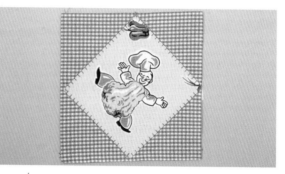

Add decorative stitching.

12. Fold under ½″ on all sides of the coordinating square.

13. Center the square at the opposite end of the towel, ½″ from the hem and 6″ from each side. Topstitch around the square.

Variation

Whether it's coffee or tea that jump-starts your day, this towel is ready to brighten anyone's day.

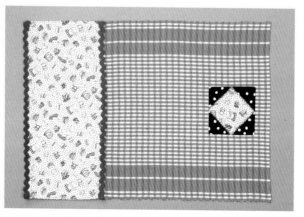

Cheery kitchen towel starts your day

creative accessories

Dream Boards

FINISHED SIZE: 20˝ × 30˝

Everyone has a dream, a wish, or a goal. And while many of us carry our dreams around in our hearts and heads, here's an opportunity to put them somewhere safe to reflect upon when you need a little visual reminder. Maybe it's a project idea or a favorite fabric scrap waiting for that moment of inspiration.

What You'll Need

- ☐ 20˝ × 30˝ × ³/₁₆˝ foam-core board
- ☐ ⅞ yard fabric
- ☐ ¾ yard low-loft batting
- ☐ ⅞ yard nonwoven fleece interfacing
- ☐ 11 yards flat braid
- ☐ Adhesive spray
- ☐ Fabric glue
- ☐ Stapler
- ☐ 18 assorted charms or large beads
- ☐ Three wire charms, such as "Dream," "Believe," "Hope"
- ☐ Metal glue
- ☐ Rotary cutter, ruler, and mat

How Tos

cutting

Prewash and press the fabric before cutting.

1. Cut a 26˝ × 36˝ rectangle from the fabric and nonwoven fleece interfacing.

2. Cut a 24˝ × 34˝ rectangle from the batting.

assembly

Note: All seam allowances are ½˝, unless otherwise stated.

1. Place the foam-core board right side up and spray a layer of adhesive on the board. Place the batting on the board.

2. Spray the top layer of batting with adhesive and position the fleece on top, smoothing the surface to remove any lumps.

3. Press the main fabric flat. Turn under ½″ on all sides and press.

4. Center the fabric on the board, placing a few pins to secure it as it is turned over.

5. Staple the folded edge to the back side of the foam-core board in the center of all 4 sides, pulling the fabric taut.

6. Continue to staple around the pressed edge, keeping a consistent tension on the main fabric. Turn the board right side up.

7. To add the braid, start on a diagonal, 4″ from the upper right-hand corner. Leave 2″ on each side to wrap to the back and staple.

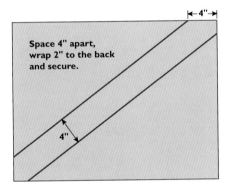

Space 4" apart, wrap 2" to the back and secure.

4"

4"

Trim application

8. Repeat the trim application every 4″ from one side of the board to the other, then place the trim in the opposite direction.

9. At each trim's intersection, hand stitch a small bead.

10. Position and glue words such as "dream," "hope," and "believe" to the board.

Variation

Teen Dream Board

What teen doesn't have her own dreams? This smaller, fun version is the perfect place to keep them close. Just add a bright, bold print with a coordinating piped trim to frame the board. A few charms placed at the intersecting ribbons create the perfect spot to keep those special dreams and mementos in place.

Too Cool Storage Stool

FINISHED SIZE: 20″ × 30″

Here's a clever thought: why not let your storage tote double as an extra seat? This two-in-one design offers a padded seat for extra company and added storage for any room in the house. Best of all, you can customize it for the bedroom, bathroom, kids' room, dorm room, or family room.

Has your sewing stash outgrown its current hideaway? May we suggest this as the perfect, concealed solution? No one will ever know your secret stash is hidden inside.

What You'll Need

- [ ] 18-gallon sturdy storage tote, measuring 16″ × 25½″ × 15½″
- [ ] 1¾ yards 54″-wide decorator faux suede
- [ ] 2¼ yards 45″-wide gingham lining
- [ ] 1 yard muslin or sheeting
- [ ] 2¾ yards fast2fuse
- [ ] 6¼ yards trim
- [ ] 2½ yards coordinating ruffled trim
- [ ] 24″ × 28½″ × 3″ high-density upholstery foam
- [ ] 1 package low-loft batting
- [ ] Electric knife or serrated bread knife (to cut the foam)
- [ ] Matching thread
- [ ] Craft or fabric glue
- [ ] Fabric and upholstery spray adhesive
- [ ] Pressing cloth
- [ ] Rotary cutter, ruler, and mat
- [ ] Air-soluble marker

How Tos

cutting

Prewash and press the fabric before cutting.

1. Cut 1 rectangle 27″ × 55¼″ of faux suede. Cut 2 rectangles 17½″ × 19″ of faux suede for the sides.

2. Cut 1 rectangle 27″ × 55¼″ of lining. Cut 2 rectangles 17½″ × 19″ of lining for the sides.

3. Cut 1 rectangle 15½″ × 58″ of batting.

4. Cut 1 rectangle 32″ × 42″ of muslin.

5. Cut 1 rectangle 26½″ × 54⅜″ of fast2fuse. Cut 2 rectangles 17″ × 18⅜″ of fast2fuse.

6. Cut 1 rectangle 17″ × 26″ from the foam using the electric or serrated knife.

assembly

Note: All seam allowances are ½″, unless otherwise stated.

1. Wrap the foam in a single layer of batting. With spray adhesive, glue the batting ends in place.

2. Fold the muslin to measure 22″ × 34″. Sew around 1 short and 1 long end. Turn the muslin case right side out and insert the wrapped foam, smoothing the batting in place. Tuck the corners into the case and glue the loose end closed.

fast!

Making a casing for the foam cushion adds an extra layer of protection while producing a more professional result. It also makes an accommodating surface for slipping the cover off and on.

3. Center the long fast2fuse panel to the wrong side of the long suede cover. Turn over and use a pressing cloth to fuse the entire length of the cover to the fast2fuse.

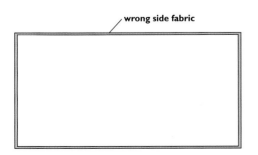

Center the fast2fuse.

easy!

When working with a dense decorator fabric, fusing may take a bit longer. Always test a small sample first for best results. If the fabric doesn't accommodate the iron well, consider using fabric glue for an easy and fast application.

4. With the fast2fuse side up, center the long gingham lining panel and fuse in place.

5. Center the long panel over the storage tote and foam cushion. Make marks on the wrong side of the cover at the storage tote corners with an air-soluble marker.

6. Place 1 end rectangle of suede wrong side up and position a small fast2fuse section ½″ from the upper, smaller edge. Fuse in place. Repeat for the second rectangle.

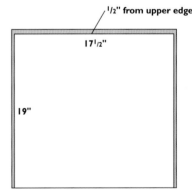

Position the fast2fuse section.

7. With the fused section facing up, place the lining on top, aligning the fabric raw edges. Fuse in place. Repeat for the second rectangle.

8. With right sides together, place the upper edge of 1 end section between the 2 marks on the long cover. Pin in place. Stitch and press the seam open. Repeat for the other end.

Attach the sides to the top.

9. Apply a row of glue next to the raw edge on the cover's vertical side edges. Start 1″ from the lower edge and continue to the top. Place an 18″ length of trim along the glue line, smoothing and pressing firmly into place. Repeat for the remaining 7 side edges.

10. Apply a row of glue to the wrong side of the ruffled trim. Begin adhering the trim 1″ above the lower, raw edges and wrapping ¾″ to either wrong side. Add a row of trim to cover the top edge of the ruffle.

11. Apply a 5″ row of glue at the upper corners. Press the adjacent sides together.

Glue the corners.

Channel Surfing at Your Fingertips

FINISHED SIZE: 13″ × 28″

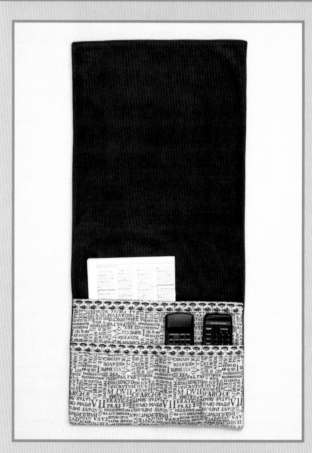

This is the perfect guy gift. What could possibly be better for him than always having the TV remote within his grasp? In this fast and easy version you'll find three pockets: one large pocket to house the TV listings; a smaller, pleated pocket perfect for hosting the remote without strain; and an additional pocket for his favorite snack food.

What You'll Need

- ☐ 1 yard of fabric A for backing
- ☐ ¾ yard of fabric B for pockets
- ☐ ⅞ yard of ½″-wide flat braid
- ☐ ⅜ yard fast2fuse
- ☐ Matching thread
- ☐ Basic sewing supplies
- ☐ Zipper foot
- ☐ Clear ruler
- ☐ Air-soluble marker
- ☐ Rotary cutter, ruler, and mat
- ☐ Craft glue (optional)

How Tos

cutting

Prewash and press the fabric before cutting.

1. Cut 2 rectangles 14″ × 29″ from fabric A.

2. Cut 2 rectangles 10½″ × 14″ from fabric B.

3. Cut 2 rectangles 7″ × 14½″ from fabric B.

4. Cut 1 rectangle 12⅝″ × 13¾″ from the fast2fuse.

5. Cut 2 strips 14″ long of flat braid.

sewing the remote caddy

Note: All seam allowances are ½″, unless otherwise stated.

1. Pin the 7″ × 14½″ small pocket pieces right sides together. Stitch, leaving a 2″ opening. Press the seam open. Turn the pocket right side out and press flat.

2. Pin a length of flat braid to the pocket's upper edge. Stitch in place.

3. Repeat Steps 1 and 2 for the large pocket.

4. Lay the large pocket right side up. Place the small pocket on top of the large, aligning the side and lower raw edges. Pin the sides only and baste together.

Pin and baste side edges only.

5. Begin at the lower left corner and pin 8″ across the lower edges. Baste to the 8″ pin mark.

6. On the small pocket, draw a vertical line from the flat braid to the lower edge, measuring 7″ from the left edge, using a clear ruler and an air-soluble marker. Stitch along the line.

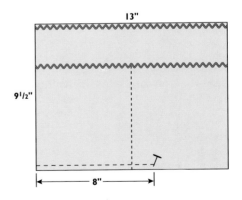

Baste along lower edge; stitch vertical divider.

7. To form a pleat in the lower right pocket, pin the lower edges together, pushing the fullness toward the right pocket's center, allowing a pleat to form. Press the fold to the right and pin in place.

8. Baste across the lower edges.

Press fullness to the right side, forming a pleat.

9. Place the pockets right side up on the right side of 1 large backing piece, aligning the lower and side raw edges. Pin and baste through all layers.

10. Place the caddy back pieces right sides together and pin along the sides and lower edges, leaving the top open.

11. Sew and trim the seam allowances. Clip the corners. Turn right side out and press.

12. Insert the fast2fuse lengthwise into the caddy opening. Position the fast2fuse in the lower half; smooth in place and fuse.

13. Press under ½˝ on the upper edges. Pin the pressed edges together and edgestitch closed.

fast!

For easier handling, why not fuse the braid in place first and then stitch?

Variation

Dorm room remote caddy

for a room of
your own

Keeping Time Journal Cover

FINISHED SIZE: 9″ × 11″

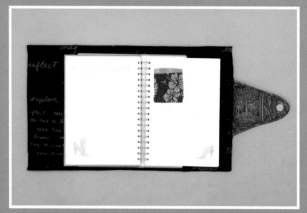

How do you keep track of your time? Whether it's a planner filled with life's upcoming activities or a journal in which life is recorded after the fact, this thoughtful wrap provides plenty of personalized softbound coverage in minimal sewing time!

What You'll Need

- ☐ ⅓ yard fabric A for lining
- ☐ ½ yard fabric B for cover
- ☐ ¼ yard coordinating fabric C
- ☐ ½ yard fast2fuse
- ☐ ½ yard ¼″-diameter cording
- ☐ One 1″ button
- ☐ 1¾″ hook-and-loop fastener
- ☐ Scrap of lightweight interfacing, at least 5″ × 7″
- ☐ Matching thread
- ☐ Rotary cutter and mat
- ☐ See-through ruler
- ☐ Teflon pressing sheet
- ☐ HeatnBond UltraHold iron-on adhesive, ⅜″ wide (optional)
- ☐ 6″ ribbon or flat trim (optional)

How Tos

cutting

Prewash and press the fabrics before cutting.

1. Cut 1 rectangle 8″ × 29″ for the lining from fabric A.

2. Cut 1 rectangle 16⅜″ × 30¾″ for the cover from fabric B.

3. Cut 1 rectangle 5″ × 6″ for the pocket from fabric C.

4. Cut 1 rectangle 11″ × 18½″ from the fast2fuse.

5. Cut 1 strip 2″ × 18″ for the bias piping from fabric A.

6. Using the Tab pattern, page 54, cut 1 each from fabric B, fabric C, and the lightweight interfacing.

assembly

1. Place a pin 5¼″ from each shorter edge of lining fabric A. Center the lining on 1 side of the fast2fuse, matching the pins to the fast2fuse short edges and leaving 1½″ of the fast2fuse beyond the longer edges. Position the Teflon pressing sheet under the fast2fuse. Following the manufacturer's instructions, fuse the lining in place.

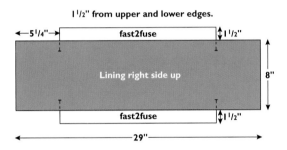

Place the lining on the fast2fuse.

2. Press under ½″ on the longer edges of cover fabric B. With the wrong side facing up, center the lined fast2fuse with the right side of the fabric on top, leaving a 2¼″ border along the longer edges. Fuse the cover to the fast2fuse.

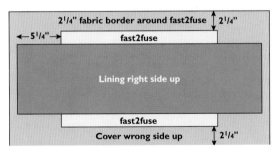

Fuse cover to liner with fast2fuse.

3. Fold the upper and lower edges toward the lining; fuse in place. Edgestitch the folded edges of the cover.

fast!

Use HeatnBond UltraHold iron-on adhesive to adhere the folded edges of the cover.

4. Fold under ½″ at the short ends of the cover. Press and fold ½″ again, covering the raw edges of the lining. Topstitch or fuse in place.

5. Turn under ½″ on the long sides of the pocket piece and press. Fold under ⅜″ at the top edge. Press and fold under ½″ again and topstitch. Fold under ½″ at the lower edge of the pocket. Press in place.

6. With the pocket and the flap right side up, place the pocket 1″ from the lower edge and ¼″ from each side. Edgestitch around the pocket.

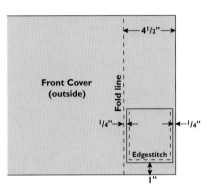

7. Fold the left cover flap 4½″ to the inside. Align and pin the upper and lower edges together. Edgestitch across the pinned edge through all layers.

8. Make a 16″ length of covered piping (see page 12). Begin with the bias fabric strip and center the cording on the wrong side. Fold the strip in half lengthwise. Use a zipper foot and sew next to the cording. Trim the seam allowance to ½″. Clip the piping seam allowance, stopping just before the stitching line.

9. With raw edges even, pin the piping to the tab lining, right sides together, along the longest edges. Use a zipper foot to baste the piping in place.

10. Pin the interfacing to the wrong side of the tab front. Baste. Pin the front to the lining, right sides together. Stitch and pink or clip the seam allowances. Turn the tab right side out and press.

11. Finish the raw edges of the tab by serging or overcasting.

12. Fold the right flap of the cover 4½″ to the inside. Press, making a sharp crease. Open the flap.

13. With right sides together, center the tab 2¾″ from the upper and lower edges. Position the raw edges of the tab just to the left of the flap crease. Pin in place and stitch along the crease, catching the tab.

Center tab 2¾″ from upper and lower edges.

fun!

Cover the raw edge of the tab by pinning a 6″ length of ribbon or trim on top and sewing or gluing in place.

14. Fold the right flap inside, aligning the upper and lower edges. Pin and edgestitch in place.

15. Stitch a decorative button 1″ from the tab's center point.

16. Apply the 2 pieces of the hook-and-loop fastener to the wrong side of the tab and opposite on the right side of the cover.

Variation

We all need a little escape from time to time. So what better way than to curl up with a good book...especially one that's under wraps?

This is an easy project that displays your favorite fabric. Simply follow steps 1-7, leaving off the piping, pocket, and tab and you've got this one under cover! How fun is that?

"Let's keep this under wraps" book cover

Sew Sensational Sachets

FINISHED SIZE: 4½″ × 4½″

Experts say that some of our favorite memories are tied to fragrances. Having trouble concentrating? Try a whiff of peppermint. Wanting to unwind? Scent the room with equal parts lavender and lemon.

What You'll Need

- ☐ At least 6″ of leopard print
- ☐ At least 6″ of muslin
- ☐ ½ yard ¼″-diameter black cording
- ☐ 1 black tassel
- ☐ Matching thread
- ☐ One 1″ black button
- ☐ 6 oz. or ¾ cup scented sachet filler
- ☐ Matching thread
- ☐ Basic sewing supplies
- ☐ Rotary mat, cutter, and ruler

How Tos

cutting

Prewash and press the fabric before cutting.

1. Cut 1 rectangle 5½″ × 10″ of muslin.

2. Cut 2 squares 5½″ × 5½″ of leopard print.

3. Cut a 13″ length of ¼″-diameter black cording.

assembly

Note: All seam allowances are ½″, unless otherwise stated.

1. Fold the muslin rectangle, short ends toward each other, overlapping 1″ at the center. Stitch the raw edges together. Pink or trim the seam allowances to ¼″.

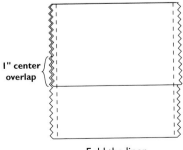

1″ center overlap

Fold the liner.

2. Fold the cording in half; bring the raw edges together and align with one corner of the back of the sachet's right side. Stitch across the edges using a ¼″ seam allowance. Add a tassel at the opposite corner from the cording, if desired.

Stitch across the cording edges.

fast!

Instead of basting, adhere the trim in place with HeatnBond UltraHold iron-on adhesive. With a seam gauge and an iron nearby, you'll have perfect trim placement.

3. With right sides together, pin the front to the back. Stitch around 3 sides, keeping the cording and tassel free. Trim seam allowances and clip corners. Turn right side out; press.

4. Open the liner and pour in the fragrance filler. Smooth with your hand to distribute evenly.

easy!

Create your own fragrance filler by mixing dry, uncooked rice, lentils, or pearl barley with several drops of your favorite essential oils in a small bag. Let the mixture dry on a paper towel to absorb any excess oil. Then fill the liner.

5. Insert the liner into the sachet cover. Stitch or fuse the opening closed.

6. Add the button to the front, stitching through all the layers.

Variation

With these fast and easy sachets you'll add a special quality to any space. Easily customized, these can be enlarged for a more generous dose or downsized and made male-appropriate with this quick version made from a recycled tie.

Suitable for a man

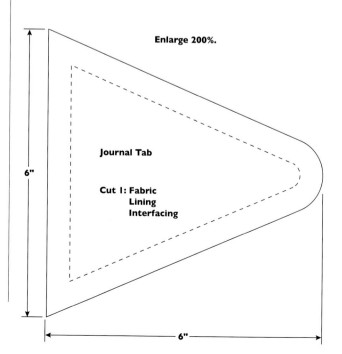

Enlarge 200%.

6″

Journal Tab

Cut 1: Fabric
         Lining
         Interfacing

6″

Author's Postscript

Creating a Personalized Space

Adding accessories to a home, whether yours or someone else's, is all about creating a comfortable, personalized space. With some quick accessory changes, a room can be refreshed or updated. The colors and fabrics chosen can add some energizing pizzazz or create a calming retreat.

Accessories can also reflect the seasonal changes with lighter and brighter colors used in the Spring and Summer while utilizing darker, richer tones for Autumn and Winter. The same home accent done in a different fabric, colors and trims will yield a very different look. And don't forget, from large to small, they're a terrific way to add your own touches to a workspace.

So whether you're accessorizing your own space or providing a thoughtful gift, try a new project or two. Begin with a favorite color or fabric and have fun mixing and matching fabrics. Who knew it could be so easy?

About the Author

Pam Archer lives in Portland, Oregon, and is a wife and mother of two sons. As a child, she loved to play with fabric scraps. When introduced to sewing, she fell in love with it.

With a bachelor's degree in clothing and textiles, Pam began her varied career in retail management. She later freelanced as national spokesperson for a major pattern company, after which she developed a high school fashion marketing program.

Presently, she is a freelance writer for *Sew News*, *Creative Machine Embroidery*, and *Clotilde's Sewing Savvy*. She is also the author of the C&T publication *Fast, Fun & Easy Fabric Bags*.

Resources

Look for home accent–making supplies at your local fabric, craft, and quilt shops. Home decorating supplies are also available from the following mail-order sources:

Clotilde LLC
P.O. Box 7500
Big Sandy, TX 7577-7500
(800) 772-2891
www.clotilde.com

JoAnn Stores
www.JoAnn.com

Nancy's Notions
333 Beichl Avenue
Beaver Dam, WI 53916
(800) 833-0690
www.nancysnotions.com

Fabric Depot
www.fabricdepot.com

The Mill End Store
9701 S.E. McLoughlin Blvd
Milwaukie, OR 97222
(503) 786-1234

3-in-1 Color Tool
C&T fast2fuse
C&T Publishing Inc.
www.ctpub.com

HeatnBond Adhesives
Therm O Web
www.thermoweb.com

Husqvarna Viking
www.Husqvarnaviking.com

Self-adhesive wastebasket
Wisconsin Lighting
www.wilighting.com

Ruthie's Rags
10602 NE Sandy Blvd.
Portland, OR 97220
(503) 261-7717
www.ruthiesrags.com